GO

BEYONDPOSSIBLE

The World's Shortest Book for Achievement, Because You Don't Have A Few Days to Make Progress and Achieve Something.

By

(David N Davis)

Table of Contents

Start Here 5

Step 1: A Clear Vision 9

Be S.M.A.R.T. 19

Step 2: Write The Vision Down as a Goal 24

Step 3 – Plan It – The Steps. 27

Enablers, the steps to Achievement. 36

Step 4 – Action - Start. 41

Step 5 – Tracking and Feedback. 46

Step 6 – Celebrate along the way. 50

Done and Dusted. 53

Conclusion. 54

Bonus Materials 57

   IKIGAI – An Introduction 57

   Types of Goals – Consider these...61

   The Importance of Dreams 64

   Alternatives or Complimentary to SMART 67
      PURE 67
      CLEAR 67

   A short comment on Age and the impact on your life plan. 69

   Areas of Life – Your Life...71

   A comment on "I do not …" Goals 74

   All the forms in one place 76

Acknowledgements 80

About the Author 81

Dedication -

Anyone who has tried to get something done and has never achieved it; to the maybe next years, next week or tomorrow, today is the day, and to myself, to see if it is possible to write a book from an idea, get it published with the help of others.

For my readers, please let me know what you got done as a result, and to those of you who did not, I have a second longer version coming out, but well done, you finished this one.

Of course, this was a secret; my family supported me in secret through this process without knowing it; thank you, Girls (Darinka, Danitsa, and Lutcia).

Thank you, folks, and thank you, Friends.

Thank you for supporting me through this journey – Doug and Pino.

To those who knew about it and read the initial versions, Doug (multiple versions - thank you), Tatiana, Ilana, Roisin – your insights and sharing was invaluable – thank you.

Foreword

In the spirit and philosophy underpinning this book, I can acknowledge that the journey of leading one's self to the achievement of your dreams and goals may be tough, it does not have to be long or complex. In fact, all you need to grasp are the timeless concepts, constructs and examples depicted so succinctly in David's journey.

In all my interactions with David, I always remember his statement that if you do not define your future, someone else will. David encourages and stretches us on our journey to make the time and have the discipline to define the future for you!

J Robison, fellow pioneer in the quest for a purpose led, fulfilling life

Start Here

"We breathe.

We pulse.

We regenerate.

Our hearts beat.

Our minds create.

Our souls ingest.

37 seconds,

well used,

is a lifetime!"

O *Mr. Magorium's Wonder Emporium*

Imagine what you could achieve in 60 seconds, 24 hours, 365 days, or 150 years?

This first section is dedicated to what the book is not; I will not be telling you about me and what I have done using the system – if you want to find out more, I have other books that detail some of these items or simply google it.

I will not tell you about the millions of people who have used the system and achieved results immediately and continue to do so.

Again that does not matter if you are not achieving anything and they have.

I will not spend pages and pages telling you why it works, all the research and experience that this comes from, or why?

Because you don't have the time, don't care, and want results. If you want me to justify how and why this works, please purchase the expanded version that will be released much later - I am happy for you to do so.

If given this book as a present to read by someone else – I am not going to conclude or draw any inferences, they likely have a sense of humor or they think you need to move out of the house or they think you need to do X or Y and they are tired of you telling them about it.

If not given this book, please buy another copy and give it to someone you know who falls into the first group.

The book is not a list of productivity tips. If you want those visits Pinterest or Google or a friend, okay, maybe I need to fill in some space later on, so I will then add in a Bonus list – but don't count on it as this is not what this book's goal to provide as a primary topic.

Some additional "if's" - if you like to argue or feel you have done this all before or there is no point - I encourage you to commit and see what happens.

Perhaps you were given the book by someone else, read into that as you want, but given this would take you about 120 minutes to read, at even15 minutes in the bathroom a day, you could complete it in less than a week, and if you don't argue, maybe you will get some value.

If you have seen this before and are not getting the results, maybe the problem is with "You" - the reader - as I know of millions of individuals who have achieved excellent results and continue to do so.

If this is you, please contact me for one-on-one coaching, as I would love to learn more from you.

Then I cannot forget the group of "I know this but did not implement it," possibly wanting to do more research before taking action - take action, do the stuff you know already, fail and keep trying; it works.

This book is for you if you have little to no time because you feel:

1. Overwhelmed.

2. Not motivated.

3. Not sure what to do, and every day seems like the same.

4. Never felt like you achieved anything.

5. You can fill more reasons below, if you must (in the space below provided):

Let us stop the small talk and platitudes, and let us get you started with achieving something, so first, before you turn this page, some practical aspects - the book is structured as follows:

1. Each part is focused on a specific step, with each piece containing a "short title" for the part of the whole; read this as summary steps,

2. an explanation for the part,

3. an example of various forms – having something, doing something, and being something types of goals (there are many other types of "goals" - I included a section on some I have come across).

4. a blank space for you to take action – even if you know this, do it anyway (I did say don't argue),

5. and space for future notes or questions or goals.

"Yes," there are blank spaces in the book.

If this is a hardcopy, use the pages provided;

If you are reading this electronically, please get a book you can write stuff down in (there is research supporting this approach – you can also order a traveler's journal) or tech-savvy and have a pencil to do so, record the items electronically.

If this is an audiobook, please do the same, buy or borrow a few paper sheets – you only need one sheet to achieve. If you are still unsure, visit my website and download a free bullet journal template - www.beyondpossible.co.za

Step 1: A Clear Vision

I once ran around an entire country, in a single morning, and followed it up with an espresso.

What are you imagining? Are you asking how? What have you assumed?

The truth is I did run around an entire country, the Vatican City, in Rome to be more specific; I also have a witness, Pino.

What is it you want to achieve?

What does it look like?

What does it feel like?

What does it taste like?

How do you feel when you have it?

Can you "see" it?

Can you picture it?

Do you see yourself doing it?

Do you see the people around you, noticing you doing it, having it, becoming it?

If someone asked you about what you see, could you explain it to them?

Can you describe it in detail?

Are you able to draw it?

Is there a video clip depicting it?

Can you edit a photo that depicts you in it?

Step 1 – you need to see what you want to achieve in as much vivid detail as possible.

Having a clear vision is the first step.

My turn with some examples.

Doing something - I want to write the world's shortest book on goal achievement because people don't have time to learn goal setting tips. The reader just wants to get to his or her destination or experience or become the result – achieve the goal.

I need a book that is between 60 and 70 pages long, minimum. The text must provide a clear and concise process that will allow someone to pick it up and read it on a flight, bus trip, or commute (if on audio, speed it up to 2x times; it is quicker still).

IT must include practical tools you can use to achieve two things; the first finish a whole book. The second accomplish a goal of your own, either a short term or a long term goal (clue – long term goals consist of many short term goals, a journey of a thousand steps starts with a single step followed by another nine hundred and ninety-nine or more – it is okay to take a detour).

I see the cover of this book.

I see it published on Amazon.

I hold a hardcopy (I have also shared it with others and have a printed copy in my hand at this very time – it is becoming real).

I see an audio version, and I see emails from people who have read and loved it, 4.5 stars.

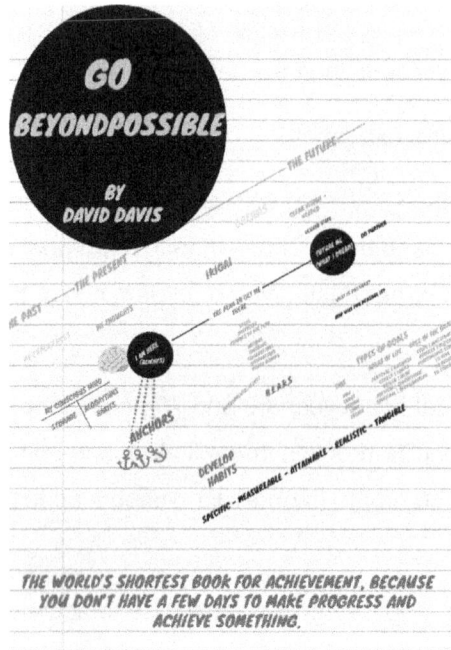

THE WORLD'S SHORTEST BOOK FOR ACHIEVEMENT, BECAUSE YOU DON'T HAVE A FEW DAYS TO MAKE PROGRESS AND ACHIEVE SOMETHING.

Does the cover look familiar?

Doing something - I have climbed (well walked up) Kilimanjaro, and I loved the experience. Once I had decided, I would attempt it (How I chose and why is the subject of another book, but yes, it involved friends, a sunny day, a glass of wine, and a "why not" question). I created a clear vision and ensured I could see myself at the top of the highest mountain in Africa, one of the 7 Peaks of the World and on most people's bucket list. I created a drawing of myself on the top.

I imagined in vivid detail the cold crisp air, the sound of the crunch of the stones under my boots, the warmth of the sun as it rose, and warmed me up.

What I did forget, though, was how I would need to get down; I did not imagine that part, odd?

Kilimanjaro

Having something – I love camping but do not have space for a large camper or trailer. My wife does not particularly like camping, as the kitchen is always a challenge. I love my wife and camping and need both.

Have you ever heard of a chuck box?

Neither had I until I was watching a YouTube video and came across a camp kitchen, scout box, or chuck box. In essence, it is a box that stores everything you need for a camp kitchen, gadgets, cooking utensils, stove, lights, and when at the campsite, the box is opened up and becomes your kitchen counter and table. It is the place to cook, prepare food, clean up and make coffee (I like coffee, so feel free to send some. If you want to produce the chuck box design, contact me; I need the royalties).

Best of all, once done, you fold it up, with all the clean (yes clean) items, pack it into the vehicle, and when home, put it away. The result is a brilliant camping experience and a happy wife, both at camp and home.

It started with an idea, which I refined until I had a precise drawing, so clear I could build it myself – that is clarity of vision when you feel you can make it yourself.

Proto-Type 2 ChuckBox Aluminium

CHUCKBOX

Cutting Sheet - Summary   Cutting Sheet D1

There are other examples, I did not have a motorcycle license, and my wife would not let me get one. Using this process, I got the motorcycle license; my wife got one too. I bought a motorcycle, and now my wife will not let me sell it? We don't need a second one, but there you go. Making use of the same process; I had a clear vision of what the bike looked like; I watched videos and saw it, I visited the stores, got on it, turned it on, took photos.

I had a clear vision – I also now have the challenge of my wife not wanting to sell it? So be careful what you wish for, as the universe has a sense of humor.

Becoming something – is often the most challenging and most time-consuming energy-intensive item to achieve. It is challenging to have a clear and concise vision of what it is to be a "better X" or the "best Y," but here is the catch, often to have something or experience something, we also need to be something.

Therein also is the clue to it all. That is how you can create a vision of "being X."

As an aside, this is often referred to as an intangible goal, as you cannot quickly feel, touch, see, hold "being the best Y" – this is again not entirely true.

You see, you can experience, feel, touch, hear being the best X. All you have to do is "see" instances where you are X. Most importantly, DO NOT say what it does not look like, what you don't want….see what you want, feel what it is and how it would appear when it is happening – no negatives.

Okay, before I lose you and waffle on too long.

I want to be the "Best Coach," so how do I create an accurate vision of me being the best coach – well, I see myself in a conversation with the head of Amazon, Jeff Bezos, after just having coached a group of 20 CEO's at my Island retreat in Brac'. Jeff happened to visit Croatia at the time, having read this book, and wanted to chat with me about how we share this with as many people globally to create a better world. Did I also mention in this vision, Elon Musk was in the group as a guest speaker – testing the Tesla submarine?

We have just finished a group session I had led, asking powerful and insightful questions, creating an atmosphere where every individual felt like it was just me and her or him in the room. They are focused. They are transforming. I am wearing a pair of flip flops, jeans, and a crisp white shirt; my Mont Blanc watch and my Travel Journal are with me (order yours now at www.beyondpossible.co.za).

That reminds me, if you know Jeff or Elon or some other celebrity or are one, give them the book and contact me – I can just imagine the initial discussion.

It is a summer afternoon;

I hear the party boat coming into the bay, playing "Ma Baker" over the speakers. The warm air touches my skin; I see the joy on my children's faces, their smiles. The crystal-clear blue water lapping up against the stones in front of the house – the house is in Sumartin on Brac'; it is a small village, and the hotel abandoned at present – but this does not deter my vision. I hear the chatter and discussion about creating a new solar power plant that will benefit villages in Africa. I am happy; Jeff is smiling; Elon is walking, the sun is going down, and I am about to walk down to the sea to swim with the girls. I am the best Coach.

Can you imagine yourself in the role? Can you feel the energy? There is no doubt; I am doing it, feeling it, living it.

My skin is prickly, it is that real.

Now a key aspect – in all of the above examples, I had not validated the vision. I did not know how or when. I knew I wanted a motorcycle, I enjoyed the experience of climbing Kilimanjaro, and I wanted to be a great coach.

I don't care if people laugh or judge me.

My vision, what I want, will become my reality.

Your turn – sketch, copy and paste, draw, cut out pictures, print copies from the web, grab a picture of yourself, and make sure you see yourself in the experience.

Please list below the other things you want, the experiences you wish to gain, or who you want to be – call it a bucket list, wish list, dream list, want list – it is your list of the future you want.

MY WISH LIST:

Do not judge what you want; or even understand how you will get there; or when, just dream the vision for now, in as much detail as possible.

Think outside of the box, nothing is too small or too big.

If you cannot select a single dream and have multiple, use the list space in the last part to capture all the dreams and wants and desires for the future, and keep adding to the list when you come across a new one.

MY NOTES OR
THOUGHTS:

MY NOTES OR
THOUGHTS:

Be S.M.A.R.T.

Before we get to convert the vision into the goal, we need to understand S.M.A.R.T.

Yes, Yes, some of you know this, but how many of you use this? Seriously, this is one example of the best advice that works and would save a lot of time and energy on your part. It is simple, so simple, yet we do not use it, do not practice it. So, for those who have seen this before and make the "not new" in the comments yet still are not achieving your goals, I would ask you to try using SMART[i].

I will also add that I have provided some alternatives in the bonus section, like PURE and CLEAR, but assume there are many more to consider – I like SMART because it is KiSS – keep it simple stupid.

I have decided to include it here and now, as will it save you a tremendous amount of time from reworking the goal while ensuring that you have a decent enough plan to begin the process.

For those of you who might not have come across this, let us spend a little time unpacking it. SMART provides a checklist we would use to ensure that the goal we set to achieve the vision is sufficiently robust and help us get there and know when we have.

S – specific – the goal needs to be as straightforward as possible; remember when we focused on the vision, describing it in vivid detail, color, sound, taste, feeling, who was with us, where and when. What was the season? What did we hear? The S emphasizes this initial key concept; the goal needs to articulate what, when, where, and who.

Some definitions of this acronym will exclude time in the specific under S.

I do not.

Being specific includes the "when will I achieve the goal," what is the target date.

Be specific.

M – measurable – this stems from the S. Assuming you were sufficiently specific, you would know how you measure progress towards the goal, and ultimately achievement, both are essential elements. Can you measure the progress you are making, either in time, distance, size, or another measurement?

In some instances, we want to become X (_____"*Insert your X*"), so if we look at the example of "being the best coach," this is difficult to measure; how do we define this and measure progress and achievement?

In the book "How to measure anything[ii]," reference is made to the measurement of intangibles – thus, how do I measure being a coach?

Well, I identify the BEAKS (another great book on competency – you can find the book in the end notes).

Another acronym.

Taken from the work of Dr. Ilana Siew[iii], in which she identifies the elements of competence or what makes an individual competent. Competency consists of various factors, namely the necessary Behaviours, Experience, Attitude/Abilities, Knowledge, and Skills. This allows me to measure if I am a great coach, as I need to be a competent coach.

I would need to demonstrate the behaviours of great coaches. I would have gained the experience of a great coach. I would need certain levels of ability and aptitude synonymous with great coaches. I would have to acquire knowledge related to coaching in the form of models, approaches, rules, ethics and other relevant aspects. I then need the skill to bring it all together for the benefit of the client.

Powerful stuff, and if you want to know more, please do read the book or listen to audio; it will only enhance your understanding and give additional insights.

As for now, just remember that the M is for measurable.

Can you accurately track and measure progress?

And do not forget to actually measure and track your progress.

A – Attainable – the goal you have described is this attainable? Can it be done? A trickier concept. It is easy to see if someone else has attained the goal, i.e., has someone else achieved a similar purpose in the past?

If "Yes," then it is attainable.

If "No," that does not mean it is "Not," but instead, you will need to work a little harder and maybe perform several other steps to achieve it.

The story of Roger Banister comes to mind, as it is cited in the literature often. The story describes how it was considered humanly impossible to run a sub-4-minute mile. The "professionals" and "academics" of the time stated this. Roger Banister himself felt he would not achieve it. His coach believed he could.

He achieved it.

A more recent example, with a similar back story, is that of Eliud Kipchogi, who successfully ran a marathon in under 2 hours - this was another feat of human triumph which many believed could not be reached - and yet it was.

There is, however, a massive difference between "not attainable" and impossible. Impossible by the very definition is not possible – I would question this, as things previously thought impossible could have been described as "we lack the current understanding at this time" versus "impossible." There are "impossible" things, and then there are many things, and maybe nothing is impossible – a scientific or philosophical debate perhaps.

Generally, our goals are all attainable; for those you are not sure about, treat them as "Yes" till proved as impossible.

R – Realistic – is with specific reference to yourself as a person, relative to your set goal. If I set the goal of being the world's wealthiest person in 12 months, this is not realistic. If I said within the next 100 years (Yes, I will live past 150 years of age, if I don't, this is likely because of some unfortunate accident or someone has wanted the farm), this is more realistic. I just have to start an idea or discover something or do something well enough to get there – there are plenty of examples of people who went from nothing to extremely wealthy, remember Jeff and Elon?

Realistic is, therefore, relative to yourself and your current abilities, resources you have, quality of the ideas and goals, how the plan fits in your broader world, the people who support you.

This is your call.

Some people will say you are not realistic;

You might say you are not practical.

You decide for yourself what this is and make a call on it. It is your plan, you are you, and it is your goal.

T – Tangible – I mentioned previously that the T is predominantly reserved for Time-Bound in many acronyms. Still, here we refer to the touch, feel, taste, experience, and hear.

The various senses.

Can you experience the goal of achieving it, or is it possible you succeed and don't even realize it?

What will you feel when reaching the goal?

What will you hear when it happens?

What would you taste when it happens?

The reason for the checklist is to ensure the goal you set provides as much detail for your subconscious mind.

Yes, I did not mention that – this system is the easiest in the world, in the shortest version as it involves the most powerful asset you have, the one you control indirectly, the one that does not judge – your subconscious.

If you set the goal and let your subconscious set up the processes for you and simply manage the results, you can achieve unique items without even thinking about it. Just remember to remind the subconscious what to do, by when and the product you want. Treat it like someone who suffers from a short attention span and will go off and explore if given a gap – do not let it.

Remind your subconscious often - morning, noon, and night.

Many books provide information on the subconscious's power, the processes, and underlying workings that drive who we are and why "we" do not listen to who we say we have to be— I would encourage you to read more on the subject if needed.

In part 2, you get to write your goal and make sure it is S.M.A.R.T.

I have included references in the bonus materials section for some other Acronyms, which can be used – PURE and CLEAR.

*MY NOTES OR
THOUGHTS:*

Step 2: Write The Vision Down as a Goal

You have established a clear vision or picture of what you want.

You need to write it down.

In the space below, write the vision down in the form of a goal.

Describe the scene you have created in your mind or drawing.

Add in more detail if you want (please use the options I have described if you are reading an e-book or audio version – I won't repeat this as you now know the possibilities. I don't want to waste your time by restating it each time, simply to fill up space and words).

It is advised to write it out and then apply the S.M.A.R.T. checklist to it, thus refining it.

MY GOAL IS TO:

MY GOAL IS SMART:

SPECIFIC – MEASUREABLE – ATTAINABLE – REALISTIC – TANGIBLE

In step One, I described the Vision of the various Goals I had and have;

I gauge their success using SMART, and this resulted in a restatement.

Below is my restatement of the Goals, all meeting the SMART criterion.

The Book – happens to be this book you are reading now – the Goal was as follows: To write my first book, with the topic of goal setting, and is less than 50 pages in length. I will have it published on Amazon within 120 days from starting to write it, thus published by November 30th, 2020.

Kilimanjaro – The goal was to climb Kilimanjaro and reach the summit while enjoying the experience before starting my MBA in February 2013.

ChuckBox – The goal was to design and build a ChuckBox that I could use for the camping trip on the 15th of March 2017. It had to fit in the jeep, provide a space for carrying all needed cooking equipment, and fold away with all contents for the next trip. Happy Wife.

Motorcycle Licence – The goal was to get my motorcycle license before December 31st, 2018. I wanted to ride the motorcycle on Chapmans Peak Drive here in Cape Town, with my wife on the back (Subsequently, I have also driven the road many times, with my Daughter on the back - a real dream come true. Danitsa - you still have not, and maybe you will now).

"Best Coach" – The goal is to host a week-long seminar for my coaches on

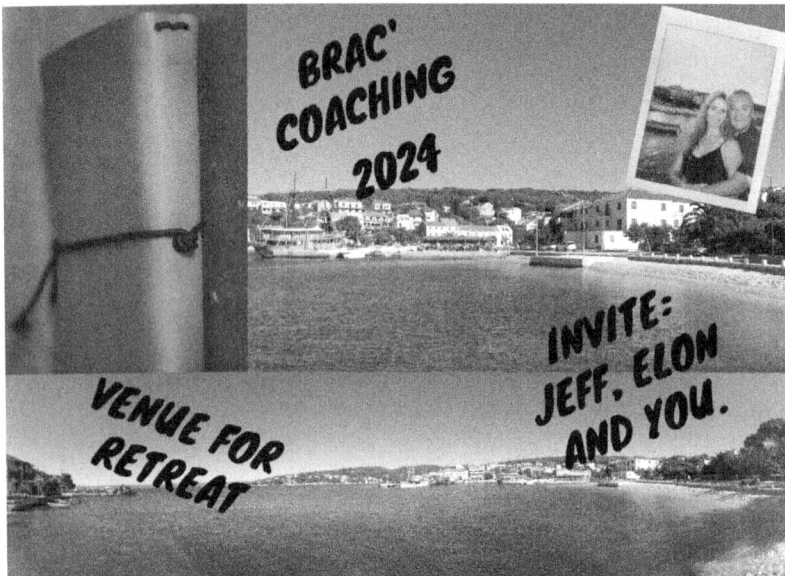

the Island of Brac in Croatia in July 2024.

Your turn again;

MY GOAL IS TO:

MY GOAL IS SMART:

SPECIFIC - MEASUREABLE - ATTAINABLE - REALISTIC - TANGIBLE

If your goal as written still does not meet the criterion of SMART, please restate it and refine it till it does.

Checkbox for SMART; tick it off if you need to elaborate more to allow your mind to ensure it is accurate.

Step 3 – Plan It – The Steps.

What?

So, you have a clear vision; you see it, feel it, taste it, and so on.

You have written the goal down and now understand the what, when, where, how, and so on.

But there is still something missing; you now have to make it happen.

That is right; I said it would be easy;

I did not say you would receive or get or have without any work on your part.

Yes, we sometimes get lucky, and do not get me wrong, I will be happy with luck, but I also know that I create my own reality and I create my own luck.

I just need to follow the plan.

Okay, so how you say?

Well, you have all you need, and what you don't have, you will go and get along the way.

What I mean is the following, since you were being developed in your mother's womb and then born, you are socialized. You are creating processes, routines, and preferences. You make and discover abilities that ultimately lead to your results. You have history, this you cannot change; it is there, it has happened.

What you can change is the future.

You do this by doing the initial steps now, using your history as a springboard into your desired future - jumping off and taking the leap of faith.

Okay, you don't follow.

Well, when you get up, you do x, y, and z or to shed more light on it; you get up, walk to the kitchen and turn on the coffee machine, take down two cups and make some coffee. While you wait, you browse through your phone.

Use these events already happening to trigger a new direction.

What? Hold on, you say? What? "I have not heard this before?"

Back to those examples, I had cited earlier.

The book – the one you are now reading – see what I did there? I am writing in front of my Mac; I do this daily as a coach. I have lots of admin, marketing, emails, articles, blogs, creativity, etc. All I have now done is slot a time to write the book and make progress - I have used what I do anyway, added a little, and presto, you have the book.

Sneak it in below the little voice in your head that says "No" or "you cannot do it" or "I don't feel like it".

Climbing Kilimanjaro – this one was a little more difficult for me at the time. I used an existing habit of reading and watching far too many YouTube videos (YouTube, you are putting in too many ads; that is why I left regular programming). I used these two skills initially to do the research, so I downloaded books of people who had climbed Kilimanjaro before, what they did how they planned it. I watched videos of individuals who had done.

As I become more proficient, I expanded my habits.

I need to get the kit, test it, so that is what I did. Using the research, I bought the equipment and then put it on and with the group went for hikes, runs, and tested the gear, even at night: All-new, but all building on the previous habits.

Those were my enablers.

How do I become a top coach – again, I fall back on reading and watching YouTube videos (still too many adds). I started to read about coaching, models, people who are considered the top coaches. Make notes, take courses, attend workshops. Watching YouTube (Evercoach is ubiquitous at present – ps. I did not like the book they consider the best, needs work – likely they will say the same about this one – but you will get results from both sources) as individuals have placed a lot of information on the site. I am now also practicing, I have a few clients, and I am writing this book as the first step – it appears top coaches all have books behind them, so why not.

All it takes is that step.

I have started talking to groups about self-leadership, such is another new skill needed to have people at the workshop on Brac' - I am available globally for these events, so do contact me.

I have already been to Croatia, and soon the family will also move there.

But the point is as follows; I am using what I already do and adding in small steps to create the larger picture – think of eating a whole cow, you would start with a little first bite; if you are a vegetarian, you begin with a tomato or two, and soon you have eaten the whole field.

Okay, now it is your turn.

You have the vision and have written the goal down.

Now you will plan the steps, working backward.

What do I need to do to get to the result?

Again, write it down. Write down the steps as they come to your mind.

THE PLAN STEPS:

Do not put numbers to the steps yet, or even dates.

Let the steps needed flow from each other, and if needed bounce around.

THE PLAN STEPS:

THE PLAN STEPS:

Next, write the steps in a sequence that you would do them in.

Now estimate the time needed to complete each step, and add the date that you intend to complete the step on.

THE PLAN STEPS: DATES

NUMBER:

These steps will then need to find a place in your existing routine habits.

What habits do you currently have and how will the first step fit into these existing habits?

Start small and link them.

In the space below list the habit and link it to the step number above.

THE HABITS I HAVE:

Okay, so now you have your steps, and I will ask the following, did you use SMART on the steps?

Is it clear what it is, what you will do by when?

Great.

Here is a question though?

Did you see any items that you don't feel are exact or are you are unsure of?

If you read the steps you have written down, will you still understand what it is you need to do, a week or two from now?

If any step does not meet this hurdle, then add to it.

It must be crystal clear what you intend to do, by when and how.

If there are still items you are unsure of, not because the step is unclear, but because you don't know how or what to do, that is great.

Note it, and then come back to it.

In some instances though, these are potential obstacles to consider.

The reality is, if you are clear on the goal and know everything, why have you not done it already? What has prevented you from achieving it already?

If nothing, then maybe it is not a worthwhile goal to pursue, or perhaps it is not a real stretch.

THE HURDLE/OBSTACLE IS?

POSSIBLE WAYS TO OVERCOME IT ARE?

What do I mean?

As I write this book, I still do not know how or who will edit it – perhaps Grammarly – why not (I used Grammarly to edit the text and also shared it with a few individuals for feedback)?

What about the cover, and then how does publishing work?

No idea, I do have the step to publish it, and because I know little to nothing about this, I will need to expand this.

I'm reminded of the Stoic philosophy based book, "The obstacle is the way[iv]" – in reality, if you run into an obstacle or hurdle, that is excellent news.

What?

Yes, great news, you know what is standing in the way of proceeding and your success, so now you understand it, find ways to overcome this, adjust the plan and make progress;

The Obstacle is the Way[i].

I realized my goal is a book of at least 50 pages, and I do not know how many words would be needed – google it - turns out about 12,500 words in total, with double spacing.

It makes sense as I am on page 18 before editing and changes inserts, and at 5500 words or so at this point – excellent, I know I can now add in some of the items I was not sure I would be able to.

I might also make the book a little shorter and ensure it is the shortest book you have read – strictly speaking if you exclude the bonus section and comments on some aspects, the book is shorter.

Quick recap, remember I said to remind the mind often and consistently, be specific; well, this recap will help reinforce the steps so far.

1. Have a clear and concise vision in as much detail as possible.

2. Write it down using a SMART approach.

3. Plan it - Identify the obstacles, add in steps, and adjust.

4. Start.

5. Track and feedback.

6. Celebrate

The summary of it all is above.

Enablers, the steps to Achievement.

You have the vision, and you converted this to goal, stated using SMART.

Part of the SMART will be the desired end date, and this is where you start your plan.

You need to work backward from this date as you build your plan.

You list the steps needed to achieve the goal, a task list, and at this stage, I recommend just listing the individual steps as they come to mind, and it is okay to bounce around and capture the steps as they come to mind.

You will find your mind creates a path towards the goal, and then as your subconscious flags the step in the plan; it will further expand in more detail for you.

Next, you place the steps in a sequence of steps.

List what needs to be done last or, if required, the first steps.

List them as they come to mind.

Next, create the series of events or tasks needed to get you from where you are now to where you need to be.

If you have all the steps, great, now attach dates to complete every step.

Suppose you need to find out information or are not sure about what needs to be completed, add in the activity to find the answer. In these instances, you will get the information and discover the necessary steps, so simply add these activities to the list you have created and estimate the time needed to find the essential information.

A plan is precisely that, it is the steps you will take to complete the necessary to deliver the result you want, but you have to arrive at a list of things to do and then add in the dates you need to complete each activity.

Depending on the level of complexity or the long term nature of the goal, you would unlikely have all the steps you need to complete it.

It is okay; just make sure you build time and activities to help identify the necessary steps.

Planning is sometimes effortless and straight forward; you know what to do and capture this in the needed detail, but sometimes you identify an obstacle or hurdle that would prevent you from moving forward or don't see a way past this. After all, if the plan were easy, we would have done it, and I would not be writing this book, and you would not be reading or listening to it.

Obstacles are a reality; there will always be something, count on it; if it does not happen, great, but if it does, do not let this derail your vision.

Simply use it as an opportunity to adjust and try something new, or try a different approach.

Here is another tip; there is a difference between persistence and stupidity.

Persistence is required to be successful.

When you feel the process will deliver results and move you forward, you should remain persistent – push a little harder, one step in front of the other.

Stupidity is doing the same thing over and over and expecting a different outcome.

Honestly, this sounds like the same thing, and the line between the two is likely evident in hindsight but not in practice.

Perhaps consider the following – when you set the plan in place, you identify items you already see as a challenge or obstacle. Use these and find a solution which either removes the barrier or block or amend the plan – yes, sometimes it is more expedient to simply go around the stone, than use a chisel to break it up into or carve the image of your noggin into it.

In some instances, you cannot go around; you need to ask if you need help. Are you not seeing the opportunity to go around or over or under, what are you missing perhaps that is not evident to you? (This is an excellent time to consider a coach – feel free to contact me directly if you do not have one)

The persistence is in the keep trying to get past, not in the how and there is the difference.

You are persistent with the long-term goal to overcome the obstacle but not in the method you are using.

Okay, my turn on the examples.

The book - I have already mentioned, I have no idea how to publish this and get it into stores, so part of the plan is to find out, Google it, and talk to people I know have published a book previously. Editing, use Grammarly, and perhaps consider hiring someone – if I have hired someone, thank you for doing this. If I have shared the book with you for comment, thank you for doing this for free.

The chuck box - a few immediate obstacles came to mind once I had decided what I wanted it look like, the functions it would need to perform, and so on. I had no tools or woodworking experience, so what did I do?

I slowly bought tools and saw it as an opportunity to learn how to use them while retaining all my fingers and toes and eyesight. Next, I did not know how the design software worked – YouTube and self-learning later, plenty of mistakes, and I was able to use design software – free as well – created the design and measurements. So now I have woodworking skills, the tools and materials, and the design.

I needed a venue, my wife was not happy when I converted the lounge into a woodworking venue, but there you have it, we all needed to sacrifice to an extent.

I then took action and learned, adjusted as I went along – refer to the next section of the plan.

Kilimanjaro - I also hinted at this previously. I was not fit, had no kit or clue, the furthest I had moved before in one sitting without a mechanical device was maybe 10 km. I intended to complete a multiday hike up the highest mountain in Africa. I found out, bought the kit, and practiced, and when the day came, I acted on it and learned along the way – and yes, I did not die, did not feel sick, and thoroughly loved it.

Okay, your turn, using the steps you set out, as many as needed in as much detail as you feel is sufficient to ensure focus and allow for the tracking to come. The goal and plan meet the SMART needs and build upon the existing you.

Do not forget to list the steps as suggested above, and yes, you have to write them down; remember writing is essential for several reasons, so let your mind go

THE HURDLE/OBSTACLE IS?

POSSIBLE WAYS TO OVERCOME IT ARE?

free and develop the plan.

Use as many sheets as are needed.

You might discover you have to complete a few different goals; again, this is great news, more clarity, and a concrete path and plan. If needed, set these individual goals and then repeat the process – I will have a diagram at the end for those who prefer a visual – skip ahead if you want also.

These individual steps are enablers.

They are the little successes and progress indicators towards the goal.

Without them, you will not progress and ultimately not complete the desired goal.

The final comment I will make is that the plan does not have to be one hundred percent complete, you need a portion only to start with, and as you go along, you adjust it accordingly. As you progress, you get new information, the universe and friends all help you along, so you might need to complete all the steps.

The other key is know what the end is.

MY NOTES OR
THOUGHTS:

Step 4 – Action - Start.

Okay, you have the vision, you have written it down, you have planned it, identified the obstacles and planned for these, all done.

Start.

Start.

Start.

Don't delay, do the first thing you can to move you forward; what is the first step on the plan you have detailed?

Do it.

Action, take action, don't delay; there will be delays, you will become demotivated, especially if the goal is a few years into the future, maybe even a few weeks.

Take action, and then retake steps as listed in the plan.

Do not stop.

Now, do you remember I spoke of the enablers? The triggers?

Even if you are the laziest slob on the planet, you have skills, operate a remote or a keyboard, and take action.

If needed, detail your existing routines, what do you do when you get up, specific points in the day, how do you add in something to move you forward today, one small step?

You are thinking, are you not?

You have started action already, now physically take action.

My example – this book, I have been writing now for two hours; I did not intend to start. Still, I had completed my work for the day, spoken to clients, did the feedback, printed the inserts for the journal, even played PS4 (sorry Xbox fans), so I had time in the afternoon before my lovely wife coming home and us having dinner. I also had not written for a week or two – truth be told, I had to dig through my index cards and find the plan for this very book.

But in all that, I took action, and now I am more than halfway written, almost nearing the end of the book.

And guess what, you are also halfway through the book – congratulations – well done, making progress, and the next section's subject.

Kilimanjaro – this involved some early mornings with friends, walking or running to build the fitness levels, visiting the camping stores, buying kit and reading, all action, and making progress. And on the day, I boarded the plane, flew to the destination, and then the next day got dropped off and started my slow walk up the mountain.

The best coach in the world – I am writing this book, am I not? I am coaching, and I am attending continuous professional development; I am looking for the needed credentialing. I finished the article for the Magazine concerning my journey (an update, this has been published for reference it was in the South African Coaching News, Volume 2, Issue 11 or visit the website for the extract). So far, my clients are delighted with the results. I know I have a long way to go, but I have this clear vision linked to a SMART goal, and I am taking the necessary steps daily to move forward.

I just realized this next step is a little more difficult for you to do well; at least write it down, but fear not, I have a solution in the next section.

Answer the following?

Did you take action? If not, what prevented it?

Okay, you know what it was; treat it as an obstacle.

You did not feel like it, well don't wait for feeling like it, that comes once you start, and if you still do not feel like it and you have worked towards it, what difference does it make?

Another clue.

If you feeling like the goal or step is not relevant or should not be considered, take action, you might then feel like it, or you might not feel like it matters little as you are making the necessary progress towards your goal. You can experience that when you get there, remember you already know how it feels when you achieve it.

So, don't worry, just do it.

Some additional comments – I need to add a few words, remember – "feeling like it" is not an excuse; starting tomorrow will never happen because tomorrow never comes. You are here now, and you can take action now, even if it is not on the plan - if it contributes to your skills to move you forward, provides additional information it is started, but also don't let this become the thing that stops the progress on the plan, take action.

Do it now.

If you have linked activities to the existing habits, you will find the patterns begin to support you further, but this would take some time. Twenty-one plus days at the very least, so keep at it, little at a time.

If you need to, get a buddy who can assist, often referred to as an accountability buddy; if none available use Siri or Alexa or a similar reminder program or app to remind you what needs to be done. If this is the case, then add a step in the plan to inform the assistant of the role and when to remind you, plus how to hold you accountable.

If needed hire a coach.

The above is a crucial concept – build on your existing habits.

Make any action you take towards the goal part of your existing routine. I have found an APP is best for this, but I also use an analog system such as the bullet journal and use the goal planner page as an example and I have a coach as well.

My view is that your history is a powerful assistant, but also a very powerful anti-assistant.

Huh?

Yes.

No matter how old you are, you have created habits, routines, and standard operating procedures. These all determine the results you get. You have reinforced these, created pathways in your brain that now efficiently and effortlessly trigger and function without the slightest action or decision on your part.

This is great as it keeps you alive but also keeps you static and safe.

But it is these same habits which can be slowly adjusted to create new routines and habits, which will result in a different outcome. This different outcome supports the steps you need to take to achieve the necessary to complete your goal.

If you can build on your existing routines and add small increments you sneak below your "safety" mechanism and develop an activity to grow you towards the goals. The reality is we are extremely good at this process. However, we create a negative spiral because we wish to be safe. So bad habits creep in because they are right, and we entrench them; but using the opposite process, thus using good habits, gets positive results. This is the same process; just the outcome has a different effect.

I would thus also include in the plan the enabler goals; these are individual habits I will develop that support my needed activities to the goal I wish to achieve.

The running example or climbing Kilimanjaro are easy examples that come to mind.

For running, I needed to stick to the plan to create the required fitness; all that was required was getting up when cold or hot, early mornings to complete the necessary long runs and invest the time. I had to do this consistently as any miss would result in a plateau that would not allow me to continue to build the needed fitness and mental strength to complete the marathon. Kilimanjaro needed the same investment in wellness and becoming familiar with the gear, and thus the same was required.

As already mentioned, I built on the existing habit of watching YouTube videos and research. I added in very short walks then runs. I added hiking and signed up for support in groups, so it became an outing versus a training session.

This all resulted in slowly building the needed fitness over time and eventually resulted in me waking up naturally without an alarm clock before dawn. Dressing automatically, and then out into the cold, crisp morning air, to start running. The rhythmic footfalls being all I heard, but being rewarded with the sunrise over the sea and the warmth and ultimately the feeling of having completed the three-hour run.

Now we get to the exciting part, tracking progress; yes, you took action and moved the needle a little or perhaps a lot; maybe you discovered help or a short cut, does not matter; you are moving forward.

MY NOTES OR
THOUGHTS:

Step 5 – Tracking and Feedback.

Okay, you have or are making progress, and you should track it.

Remember the plan; the simplest way to track is to cross off the line items as you progress.

But there are as many other ways to track specific items as there are pizza types and many more created daily.

In my examples, I used the following tracking methods:

The book – I continuously look at the number of words and number of pages – remember this is supposed to be the world's shortest achievement book, and thus I set the goal to create a 40 to 50-page book, which translates to about 12,000 words. At this stage (before editing), I have 37 pages in total and nine thousand three hundred and thirty-three, four, five; you get the picture. I also wanted to get this book written before the end of October and then published before Christmas.

Now, remember, I do not have a cover or know how to publish, but the plan did have items that allowed me to overcome this.

The cover of this book - I have turned to Fiver and will identify a provider here for this. The publishing was a little more cumbersome, so I have attended an online talk, I have downloaded a course on publishing a book on Amazon, and I am working through this in parallel.

A pivotal point to mention, you can decrease the time to achieve the goal by working in parallel; in other words, do what you can and learn as you go along. The different approach is to outsource activities; for example, I will outsource the cover creation to a professional, even though I am proficient in Canva.

Kilimanjaro – as we were in a group and we had a deadline date to be on the mountain and execute, we had a checklist and ticketed these events off as we completed them. We also continued to do things in parallel, like research, gear testing, and plenty of coffee and wine, a few lunch and learns, have some fun – the subject of the next section.

Marathon – I used Nike Running APP for this and my smartwatch, which then captured all statistics I needed to cover the required plan I was following. Again I had a deadline, but a concept I had built in was to meet certain milestones before attempting the marathon.

This is another consideration in your plan.

Do build in some milestones that provide a go- or no-go decision point, especially where you are unfamiliar with or require significant investment in time and resources. I thus had identified a need to complete a training run of at least thirty-two km at any time midway towards the goal and then also a thirty km race event within a specified time. These would provide the necessary confirmation my training was on schedule and build confidence towards the ultimate 42,2km (yes, those two hundred meters at the end are the best, and without them, you do not complete the marathon).

Chuck box – here I used the checklist approach, ticking off as I progressed, and then once I started the build, I could see the progress as I cut pieces and glued them together – by the way, I use this approach now with the leather projects I have recently started to pursue.

Motorcycle – again, checklist against the plan, each stage being ticked off and completed as I progressed.

The coaching event is long-term. Here, the plan is not entirely developed – I have a long-term goal of many milestones, some unknowns, but I have sufficient to start and work towards the dream. I have a checklist, which involved becoming an accredited coach – done. Build a client base – in progress – as I begin to develop programs and packages, I have annual goals and targets for revenue, income, hours. The book is part of this process, and I am writing.

There are two key concepts to consider from the above: one, you do not need a complete 100% detailed plan (I hinted at tis earlier on), and you might need plans and goals within plans and objectives (By the way, I am on page 38 now - progress).

You do not need a complete 100% plan in detail; all you need is the end vision and then the initial steps to bring you closer. As you did not know, these steps might initially not be required, which is very real for many goals. Do not see this as a deterrent, but rather part of the foundation and learning that get you to the final destination. You might complete items that do not directly contribute to the goal. If this happens, see it as the learnings, and learning do contribute to the plan.

These initial steps are needed, so you have something to start and build upon; much like building a house, you create the foundation and then add and change as you go along, and sometimes you add to the foundation, but very seldom do you take away.

Plans within plans and goals within the goals, especially true for big dreams, as you will not know or have all you need to achieve the final objective. You will need to complete the milestones, and these can be goals in themselves. The house analogy holds here. You have a house plan, but there are electrical, water, sewage, garden, and other projects as you go along. All have specifications and details and steps to complete in the sequence needed to contribute to the overall final result.

The same is valid for life goals.

Back to tracking methods, you can use any of the below and then feel free to create your own:

- Graphs

- Journals

- Photo records

- Thermometer diagrams.

- Plot charts.

- Checklists.

- APP.

- Etc.

- Etc.

The tracking aims are three-fold – firstly, it will help maintain the focus by reminding you to track what you feel is essential, but doing so allows you to progress.

Secondly, it provides feedback on the timing and adjustments needed. Use it to help you remain on track and, if required, make adjustments to the plan going forward.

The third item it provides is the opportunity to celebrate, another critical aspect to maintain your motivation. As you make progress, you build confidence, and celebrations help you retain this and share the progress with your support.

What you cannot measure, you cannot track and cannot manage.

MY NOTES OR
THOUGHTS:

Step 6 – Celebrate along the way.

Extremely important to celebrate along the way.

Goals you have set can sometimes make you feel like you are not making the needed progress.

For the last few years, I have made use of Leadership Management International's materials. Thus, I use the definition of success we teach to delegates who attend our programs - "success" is defined as the progressive realization of worthwhile, predetermined personal goals (All credit of this definition to Leadership Management International[v] - please visit the website for more information, you will not be disappointed or contact me for a discussion on how these programs allow you to achieve your potential).

A component of the definition is the focus on progress towards versus achievement of the dream?

More often than not, when I work with a group and seek definitions of success or a description of success, the vast majority of attendees list success in terms of achievement. They either have something, own something, have done something, or some similar terminal result.

Very few, if any, define success as the journey.

Remember the saying, life is a journey or success is a journey, not a destination.

Enjoy the ride?

Wonder why that is.

If you are making progress towards your goal, the end, the vision you have created for yourself, you are successful.

You cease to become successful when you stop pursuing the dream, either because you have achieved it or because you have given up. You have reached it; you were successful. You did not complete it; you were not successful.

If you continue to pursue the dream, you remain successful, as you are progressing towards this dream.

The other concept is that of motivation.

You see, we often lose momentum, and to remain on the path, you need to celebrate the small steps and victories.

I might have mentioned that a year ago, I ran my first marathon – I smile as I know I have mentioned it, a few times.

The goal was to run the marathon in six to six and a half hours (by the way, I finished in six hours and fifteen minutes - odd considering the goal?) and have fun doing it. I trained for months, slowly extending my running and walking. I distinctly recall reaching the 32 km mark during the marathon, for two reasons.

The first, my mom phoned me and asked what I was doing - I still smile at this. I did mention I was running a marathon, but this had slipped her mind, so we ended up chatting while I was running along. Very casual, but it got me through those steps – and I remember where I was on the route.

The second, when I reached 32km, I realized that every step I took towards my goal of completing the marathon was a step further than I had ever run before. I was in pain, and my legs were sore, and yet I was smiling, as every step I took was a step further than my previous best.

I still get goose bumps when I think about that.

I celebrated every step,

Goals are made up of steps and milestones - celebrate these and record them.

The steps provide the necessary motivation for you and also a record of the progress for tracking purposes.

The celebration is essential to maintain your motivation and show the progress will continue to reinforce the subconscious that this is important and can be achieved.

Celebrate as often as can, provided you make progress.

List a few ways you will celebrate below.

Done and Dusted.

Congratulations, you have completed this book, well at least the reason you decided to read it or why someone gave it to you. Of course, you can continue to review the tools I have included below and some of the additional links and resources.

But for now, well done, you set out to read a book in less than four hours, and you have achieved this.

Maybe, you were using an audio version and did not speed it up. Why not? You could likely have done this in less than 2 hours.

Of course, I say reading, remember to be specific as possible; you likely spent more time if you did the exercises I have included, but if you have done so, well done as you will reap additional rewards.

If you simply read the content and did not do the exercises, please do them. There is significant research which supports the onboarding of knowledge is significantly improved when you see, hear and do.

How many books or great ideas do we come across daily, and we never take action to embed them.

When I started the book, I referred to those who had seen this before and simply said "Yes, I know" and read through and then did not take action to use the information and apply the data they had to create knowledge benefit.

Yes, I am talking to you; if you read this or listened simply to get through great, I did the work by writing this for you and allowing you to read it, but if you did not take my advice and write it down, take the steps, please go back now and do so, work through it.

Set the first goal for yourself and work through it.

Conclusion

I have not mentioned yet that this book is a secret; the family does not know I am writing it, yes others do know, as it is part of the planning I put together with my coaches when embarking on the development for 2020.

2020 has been a year that has allowed us to relook what is essential and our role in the world. It has allowed us to put things aside; we might have lost people we know, loved ones, jobs, and other norms.

I am sorry.

In this, however, we can create something we find is significant, and I hope this book and process will contribute to this future, which is more of your reality, what you want.

You see, because we are creatures of habit, only a significant event shakes us out of the approach. The COVID-19 events have done precisely this. It has affected every person on the planet in some way or another, directly or even indirectly. Much like what I imagine a world would have been like during a world war. This has been both an opportunity to relook and reconfigure, and thus the steps I have suggested will help you develop this new world for yourself and others.

What have you done during this period?

Did you use it?

If not, this book should help you.

Thus, as a reminder, do the following:

1. Dream, dream big, or dream small, but do dream and write these down, draw them create pictures of them, feel them, experience the joy; as I am writing this, use this to make the Vision of what you want.

2. Write it down – let me repeat that, write it down; you have twice as much chance of getting it if you write it down. Write it down, and remind yourself of it, use the SMART test.

3. Plan it – set the steps required within the process to get you from the point you are now to the place you want to be, to the memories you wish to have and to the person you want to become.

3.1 Enablers – build on who you are and what you already do. Be sneaky; remember your brain is designed to keep you alive, and any change is a threat, so sneak it in there, slowly and in small pieces. We all move mountains, just a handful of sand or rock at a time.

4. Action – you have all you need, even if you don't believe it or even if you know you don't, get it on the way. A long journey requires detours, stops, and rest to complete it, no one can do it alone, and no one can go all the distance of the vision of a better world without taking breaks and refuelling. But they all start; you eat an elephant with many small bites, and a journey of one hundred thousand steps begins with the first step. Take the step.

5. Track your progress and get or give yourself feedback – this will ensure you remain on track; highlight any changes you need to make. Provide the support and advice you will need.

6. Celebrate – often; celebrate as you progress; it provides motivation, opportunity to share, and enjoy the journey along the way.

Congratulations, you have completed the book and now take a break. More importantly, if you can apply the seven steps to all goals, you will live a happier life— one filled with achievements and, more importantly, filled with your accomplishments and memories.

Please do send me a note and share your experience, and as this is the social era, please post a comment on the review section, share the book with others and recommend it; in other words, please like, subscribe and share.

I would love to hear how you have used the material in this book – send me a note at beyondpossible@beyondpossible.co.za.

Thank you, and good luck.

Bonus Materials

I have included these to allow you to explore some additional concepts. Each on their own could be a separate chapter or book, requiring years of research, but do consider them or don't, your choice entirely; after all, you have already completed the book's goal.

IKIGAI – An Introduction

So what does Ikigai mean to those of you who have not come across it before?

Well, simply put, Ikigai means to live your life purpose, which implies you know what your "purpose" is?

Ikigai is a Japanese word that consists of two different words to create a single unified concept – "Iki" means "to live" and "Gai" means "reason." Thus "to live with reason" or "life's purpose."

My Traveller's Journals are stamped with the word "Ikigai."

The second and for me as critical is the hypothesis proposed by Francis Galton. The suggestion that any culture or race personality or trait once embedded within the culture is reduced to a single term – in this case, Ikigai. An example that comes to mind is the term "Now Now" (yes, not a single word, but a South African who uses the term referring to time will understand its meaning. A non-South African will not (If interested, the term describes when someone would do something. "I will be at the house Now Now." should be understood as possibly 5 minutes to 5 hours or even later. Be warned if you hear this term, request specifics immediately.)

The inference I draw is that because many cultures do not have a single term for your own life's purpose, is it no wonder we struggle to articulate and identify it in the first instance?

Thus we would naturally lack the first requirement – clarity of vision.

No wonder we spend a lifetime trying to determine what our "purpose" is; very few of us discover this and live happily ever after?

When I think of master craftspeople, irrespective of their country of origin, the artists they are living their Ikigai, for them, this is not perceived as "work." I recall watching a video on braaing or for others BBQ'ing.

The video has a segment where this individual speaks like a philosopher, describing the link between nature and people, his reverence for the trees and forest. Initially, I could not work out what the individual did, and then they finally share it – he makes charcoal. I was stunned; there was an individual who treated charcoal – something I buy at the supermarket or local fuel station and think very little of, except for will it stay hot enough for me to cook my dinner. This individual saw creating the best charcoal as his sole purpose. He was an artist, and the film goes on to show how his charcoal is used in the top restaurants and globally sought after – wow (if someone can tell me how to get a copy of the film, I would greatly appreciate it).

Imagine you can discover this for yourself? Imagine that you are working every day to execute this, and the result is you live a longer, happier life?

What?

Yes, it is now scientifically accepted that individuals who live the longest and healthiest lives, with little to no stress, have discovered their Ikigai. A 2008 Osaki Public Health Study and on the Island of Okinawa, Ikigai is attributed to the individuals' quality of life and longevity.

Food for thought.

I use the Father Christmas principle; you can apply this to the Easter Bunny and Tooth Fairy. If you don't believe in either of these characters, you are 100% guaranteed not to benefit from the experience. If you do believe and support or play along, you do get presents and easter eggs. If you lose teeth, possibly some cash reward depending on the current market rate of used teeth.

I apply the same to Ikigai – I can dismiss it and then possibly not benefit, or I can actively pursue my Ikigai and perhaps benefit while being happy and content – sounds perfect.

But how?

Fortunately, others have distilled some key questions – do a quick google or YouTube search or even TEDx talk, and you will find 100's, so this is not new, yet we don't? Does this sound like the comments made earlier on?

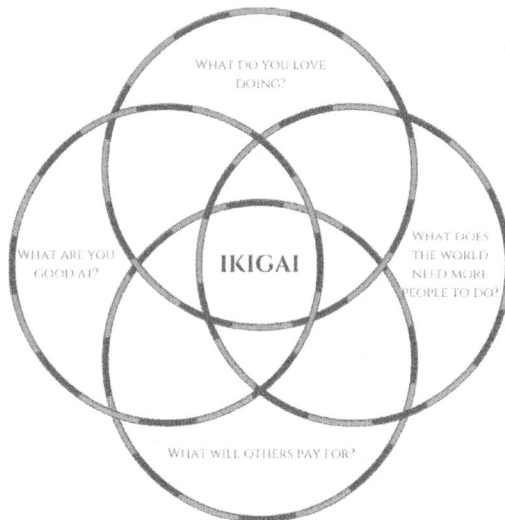

FOUR ELEMENTS OF IKIGAI

Ikigai - "Iki" means "to live" and "Gai" means "Reason."

Your Ikigai is your reason for living.

Ask yourself these questions:

1. What do you love doing?
2. What are you good at?
3. What are others prepared to pay for?
4. What does the world need more people to do?

BEYONDPOSSIBLE

WHAT DO YOU LOVE DOING?

WHAT ARE YOU GOOD AT?

IKIGAI

WHAT DOES THE WORLD NEED MORE PEOPLE TO DO?

WHAT WILL OTHERS PAY FOR?

The above diagram is a summary, and as an example, here is my very own Ikigai – which has taken me a few years to discover.

I am a coach; I love coaching individuals and teams, which results in a better world. The world needs people who can coach and develop others; I am very good at coaching, with clients reminding me and seeking my coaching services. I also get paid by these individuals to coach, and I have the flexibility for creativity, like writing, leatherwork, family time, and many other pursuits.

I have purposefully followed a format, as this allows you to discern the questions, and I would encourage you to answer these for yourself.

1. What do you love?
2. What are you good at doing?
3. What does the world need more of to benefit from?

WHAT DO YOU
LOVE?

WHAT ARE YOU
GOOD AT?

4. What will others pay to get?

WHAT DOES THE WORLD NEED
MORE OF TO BENEFIT FROM?

WHAT WILL OTHERS
PAY TO GET?

A common question raised by individuals, who wish to clarify and categorize the goals, is what types of goals are there?

The categories do provide for a level of analysis and provide you with the essential questions to ask yourself, but in no way should you feel like you have to have every type of goal listed.

For this book, you must just set a goal and go for it.

Do not worry about the category; simply develop the goal and begin; this is significantly more important than classification.

If you genuinely feel you would like some background and additional understanding, I have shared some of the goal types I have come across, but a google search will again provide the needed answers.

Based on my experience, all goals can be classified into various groups, such as length of time, area of life, or goal type.

Time-based classifications are based on the length of time estimated to achieve the goal?

Now, short-term, medium-term, long-term, and legacy goals (this is not an exhaustive list) all describe the length of time relative to a specific aspect. For example, a short term goal for one person might be a medium-term goal for another.

You decide if short means one day or one week or one month, does medium refer to a quarter or half-year, does the long term refer to one year, five years, ten years or even longer, perhaps you have a lifetime goal. In some rare instances, an individual would develop a legacy goal, this is a goal that can only be achieved once the individual or generations of individual passed on.

Have you considered a legacy goal?

Area of life goals refers to the "where" of the goal versus the "when," which is time-based. "Where" would also include goals for others, the "who" of your world. I have included a chapter on the areas of life; however, it is essential for resilience. With the ability to deal with adversity, and to ensure balance in one's life, thus I encourage you as the reader to establish the areas that work for you and set goals in each of these areas.

An additional classification uses the role the goal plays in the process or plan?

Thus you could have a steppingstone goal that provides the immediate steps towards a more extensive or longer-term goal. It is the achievement of the plan's small actions that result in progress and provide for the needed points of celebration.

Milestone goals provide for additional points along the path of the desired plan towards the achievement. Milestones are different from stepping stones in that they usually are made up of several smaller steps versus milestones, which refers to the completion of a segment of the plan.

Process related goals refer to the successful establishment of the process overall to achieve a goal and indicate establishing a routine or habit that contributes towards the longer-term goals. I say long term as usually any habit to be broken and re-established may require a minimum of twenty-one to sixty days to achieve success. An example of this would be the habit of getting up early; the 04:30 am club members would relate to this, where getting up is the start of a defined routine that leads to effective habits and sets up your specific day.

Typically we associate all goals with an outcome.

These outcomes can also be categorised.

Even more common are the goals to have something or experience something, the type of goal we often fail to seek out are goals I describe as "to become" goals.

To have goals are often easily identified as you can visualize and experience the item you wish to have, perhaps a new car or home or shiny object. The "too experience" goals are related to travel, playing a game, having an experience.

The "to become" goals are less common, as this involves the change in habits and ways of being, changes in your behaviors, and are often required to be successful in the other goals, but more often than not, are entirely ignored.

Performance standard goals establish a minimum expected level of performance; these goals are associated with milestones to achieve an item and rely on setting the desired minimum levels of performance.

The formation of "to be" goals - you should have an idea that types of goals all form part and parcel of the more considerable ultimate achievement you wish. You have to become someone else to have and when you experience, you do become someone else – you grow.

Do not get bogged down in the types, but where they will be of value is to discover what is holding you back from achieving the desired outcome, and thus as you work back down the ladder, you might find you need a milestone step or process.

That reminds me, you only know if you are making progress if you measure and track your goals progress. Tracking your performance relative to the goal provides you with feedback and allows you to adjust and seek out ways to overcome what is needed to keep you moving forward on the goal.

This is a critical step in the process.

I have included a diagram below clarifying where the various goals and description of goals find themselves, and I am sure there are 100's more. I would encourage you to share these on the website beyondpossible.co.za.

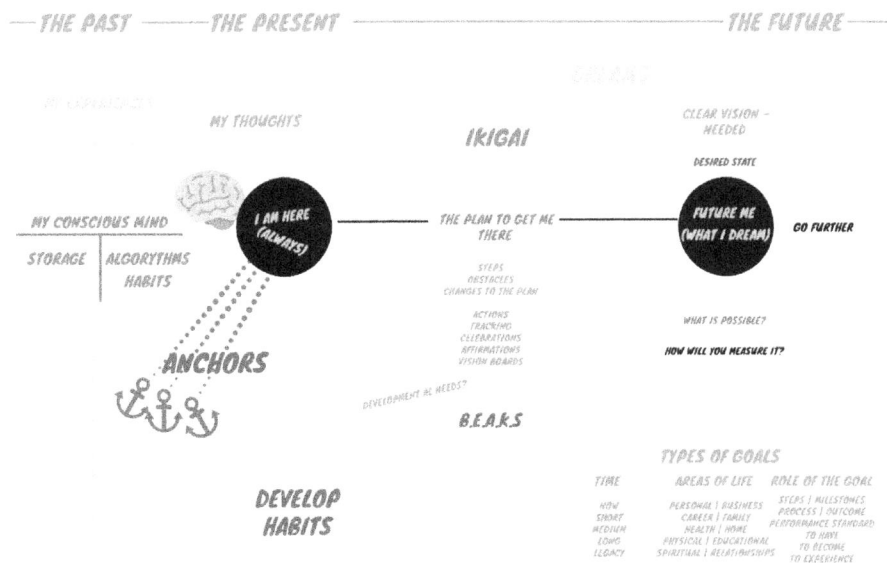

STEP | PROCES | HABIT | PERFORMANCE STANDARD | OUTCOME | TO BE | TO HAVE | TO EXPERIENCE

The importance of Dreams cannot be overstated.

I have lived in a number of countries due to the nature of the work that I do. Unfortunately, I have also witnessed the absence of Dreams of the future; this is also extensively listed in Viktor Frankl's book, "Man's Search for Meaning," where he details accounts of individuals who lose hope, and the resultant death of these individuals. In one or two of these countries I would be negotiating for a future gain, and I was always saddened to see some individuals take a fraction of something today as they could hold onto it and control or use it, even if tomorrow brought double in some instances.

I attribute this to the same reality; without dreams, you simply live the same repeatedly, or even worse, you live for someone else, doing what you could for yourself and not for others.

You have to have a dream and you should dream big; in our programs, we use a dream list, call it a wish list (and "the secret", much like in "The Secret" is that these come true, if you do some of the work); In our programs, you compile a list; you write down and continue to add to the list as you go along. It provides you with the necessary input for potential goals when you achieve the immediate goals you have set for yourself.

Thus, I would encourage a similar practice, create a list of dreams, and here is the key in doing this, do not under any circumstances apply logic to the list, so let me share two stories to illustrate this.

The first, on my list, is this book, so do not laugh, but also on my dream list is my trip to space, and when I shared this with my wife initially, well, let me put it this way, I love her dearly, but yes I did not feel the support, to be honest. She simply laughed, and in that is the one element to remember, this is your list, so don't worry if anyone thinks it is not achievable, reasonable, or other reason it is not possible. Simply put it on the list and remember if you share it and people laugh, see this as you are on the right path.

If you know of anyone who will sponsor the trip or how I could achieve it on the dream list still and I don't know how, but it is there. If you wonder, I might not take my wife with on the trip, although I likely will just laugh while on it, this time with her and not at her.

The second is I had a client who had signed up to complete the program, and the exercise was to create your dream list. She showed up at the session and presented me with a blank page?

Really.

A blank page? (I know she knows who she is, and some others also know who she is).

Well, this would not do; I explained the criterion, and she resisted.

So, I said, "okay, I am going to the bathroom; when I get back, I want to see something on the page, does not matter what, just anything you dream of. I don't want to know how you will achieve it or even when, just what it is."

And off I went.

When I returned, she had written almost a page and continued to add.

This is common for many individuals. Once they start, they don't stop; I had one client who wrote six pages of dreams; well done.

Now here is the reality of this story; within six months, she had achieved two of the items on the list, and this last month, she moved into her new home, which was also on the dream list.

She has continued to add.

But a word of caution, and I would have shared this before, the universe has a sense of humor, so be careful what you wish for and when you do, be specific; the universe is also sneaky, so be as detailed as possible.

The take away is to create the dream list.

Do it now if you have not done it already, take a piece of paper or even better, grab a journal (if you need a format, visit the www.beyondpossible.co.za and download the one you can use, or order the journal, handmade leather traveller's journal) and start writing.

If this is a hard copy, use the space below to start the list, remember this is what you want, don't worry about how or when, do not apply SMART, please don't as your list will be concise, and you will be depressed.

So, write, dream, imagine; what if you won the lotto, what if you did this? Where do you want to go, who do you want to meet, what experiences do you want?

Write.

Write.

Write.

DREAMS FOR MYSELF

If you need more space, grab some extra sheets, or better put it into the journal you bought from our website.

As an aside - I am now on page 43 completed, remember the tracking element, and 12,589 words, sorry ninety-one, three, five to be exact.

As with many acronyms in use in any field, there are usually many alternatives, and I, therefore, encourage you to seek the ones that you feel add value to you personally, and ultimately encourage you to remember, act upon, and make progress.

A google search will bring up several options to consider; the below is by no means definitive but does provide for additional and independent checks that one's goals are appropriately set.

PURE

P - Pure - I wonder how much there was a need for the "P" to create the acronym of PURE? The goal must be PURE; perhaps the P is to remind you of the next 3? Not sure, but maybe we should substitute the "Pure" for "precise" - the goal must be precisely stated, clearly stated, and to the point.

U - Understood - Understood? Yip, in the law, there is a concept that when people agree on anything, there is an underlying understanding that they agree to the same thing? The implication is they understand what and why? They know what the goal is, the impact, and can commit to the performance soundly. Do you remember the section on the plan, where I asked if you would remember what you had stated as the step a few weeks later? This is why, if it was clear, you will still understand it.

R - Relevant - seems this is common sense, but appears not. The goal must be relevant (SMART refers to this), appropriate to the person whose goal is being performed by and to those who will benefit and judge the goal. If it is not relevant, what is the point essentially?

E - Ethical - this is a philosophical aspect; depending on your approach and definitions, this is open to interpretation, but do make sure it fits your ethics at the very least.

CLEAR

C - Challenging - is the goal challenging enough? Often we will set a goal based on the person we are now and feel we can become in some future state. This goal is limited as a result. Thus, it is suggested that you set a goal in the typical fashion and then add to it, not by shortening the time but by what you intend to achieve.

For example, if you intend to run a 5km race, set the goal and training for this, but why not make it 6km.

The 10%-20% rule can be applied.

L - Legal - always ensure the goal is legally permitted in the area you wish to perform the goal. The key here is that what is legally permitted in some countries is not necessarily lawfully allowed in others. Just check this.

E - Environmentally appropriate - should extend beyond the simple nature and planet test. The word here is to be seen in its broadest possible use. Thus, it would rise to your social environment, legal environment, and biological environment; in other words, apply the environmental test to all the settings you find yourself in.

A - Agreed by all parties - a goal that involves others and is dependent upon their cooperation, and truly stretch or big goals are always to some extent, make sure you have their understanding and buy-in. If this is not agreed upon, understand why it might yield some information that would be relevant and important to consider.

R - Recorded - this is a reminder to make sure it is captured in ink. How often have you set a goal and then not followed through and, in some instances, perhaps wholly forgotten it was a goal? Here is a great example; for years, we had the tradition to write down our new year's goals and then burn them. Yes, it was cool to do this and always fun, but we could not remember two or three days later.

Write it down and display it somewhere; create the vision board if needed (if not sure what this is, Google or YouTube).

Whether you consciously have a plan or don't, we all have a life plan – the idea of what a great life would feel and be like to us.

In my case, it was something like this; you are born, you then go to school at some point, once completed my plan required me to go to university and get a degree. At some point, I would get married, have a few kids, buy a house, move up the career ladder, eventually retire, grow old, and die.

This plan also had some built-in assumptions of age; you see, school starts at 5-6 years old and finishes at 18-19 years of age. University or college would follow for 4-5 years. Get a job and then married by 30, with kids by 35 and then career growth for the next 25 years until retirement and life enjoyment.

You likely have a similar plan, which might be a dream of yours – this is not a comment or judgment, but there are an assumption and measurement or comparison embedded within this, implications.

If you are not married by age, don't finish school, don't have children, don't have a job, don't have the house compared at the age of 50 expectations, you have not achieved.

What if, like myself, you will live to 150, at least?

What now, can I change my educational degrees, so what if I don't have the house, or did not visit this place or that by 45? What if I did not get an educational degree by 20? Can I get one at 75? Can I change my career at 90?

What if?

How does this change the plan?

Do you now have options?

Are you worried when you have not met the plan?

Age is the one aspect we should change as it will make a significant difference in your life choices.

Can you dance in the rain when you are 40? Some people do, most don't because it is childish?

I do realize this is a very selfish view of the life plan. I cannot compare to others who have not been as privileged as I have, even to pursue a dream of this nature. Still, irrespective of the society you find yourself in, I am 100% there is an acceptable time line for where and what you have achieved at certain points.

It all presupposes and results in comparisons and assumptions.

MY NOTES OR
THOUGHTS:

At this stage, you might start to consider which goal comes first, priorities, and possibly feeling overwhelmed. That is to be understood, as which one should I pursue first, how do I decide?

One approach is the Areas of Life; this is a fairly common item used by coaches to help individuals segment, measure and manage any change they anticipate, but more importantly, it has implications for happiness and resilience (Significant research is available on this).

The concept is as follows: if you have a well-rounded life; a balanced life; thus, all your areas are functioning at the optimum levels you have established and none of them are neglected or more robust than others; your life is like a wheel; it will roll easily, it is balanced. If this is not true; you have a square or mishappen wheel, which will not move as well, as effectively. It will take more effort, more energy.

Does this sound familiar, constantly tired, exhausted – look at your areas of life.

You also have to decide which areas of life work for you, and how many?

I would suggest it is entirely within your remit, although many views are indicated on this, along with why this is better than another.

At the very least, I would suggest you have two areas, one related to personal items the other your work-related, career-related, for example? If you do not have a career, you have a personal life;

I would still suggest you segment this somehow.

As an example you could segment it into "my time" and "other time", health, etc.

In some instances, I have come across eleven areas; when completing my Masters of Business Administration, we looked at eleven areas of life. Prof. Kurt April had an assessment tool for this. If you need others, perhaps six, we use six areas in LMI programs, while I recently saw Ever coach referred to 6.

I have 7, based on the 6 Leadership Management International, and where I split one of the areas.

Some suggested areas could include but would not be limited to the following, and you create the definition to define the area, so Spiritual means one thing for some and another for others.

Remember, there is no wrong or right, like your dreams list; this must work for you and you alone. Still, it does help if there are some consistency, as you can learn from others, and also, it would assist in the development of the goals and potential synergies have, or my favourite working in 3 or 4 areas at the same time.

For example, when I go for a run, I also listen to motivational materials. When I drive and listen to audio books, I am working on my business, self-development, health, and others. I also run in a group with friends, so another box ticked.

Examples are thus as follows:

- Personal.

- Business.

- Career.

- Family.

- Health.

- Education.

- Spiritual.

- Financial.

- Home.

- Social.

- Cultural.

Feel free to add your own, and if you do, be consistent with your definition.

I have to mention the above; we often know what we don't want, what we don't want to do, and what we don't "whatever."

We are extremely good at stating these "non-existent" items.

When setting goals, you must affirm them; much like the vision and the affirmation, they must be positive - an image by its very nature exists and is visible.

What?

What do I mean?

In a nutshell, our minds have difficulties when we imagine an absence of something (maybe meditation by a yogi or similarly experienced practitioner), as Descartes put it, "*Cogito Ergo Sum*" or "I think therefore I am." You see, in thinking we exist, and thus when we set a goal not have, or to lose weight, or not to procrastinate, or not to talk ugly to people, or not be a whatever, we inadvertently picture it and try to create the "not" part.
We all fail at this.

By "not" wanting X, we imagine X, so we create X.

The key is to picture the result of what "not" doing X looks like.

For years I have weighed a constant 100kg's and would try to reduce this by setting the goal to lose 5kgs.

See the "loose" portion of the goal?

I don't like to lose anything, so why would I lose the 5kg's? But when I set the positive goal to weigh a specific weight, guess what, I know what 95 kgs look like, what it feels like, and I have not lost anything; I have gained something.

Let me try another example; a client of mine is currently grappling with this case; refer to him as me, so I am now grappling with a need to develop my confidence. I feel that sometimes I picture myself as small in others' presence for various reasons; there is no reason to feel this way; after all, I have done more than most people will dream of, and I will do much more.

The question is, how do I set a goal of being confident?

What does this look like?

I know what it does not look like, feeling small, not speaking, holding back, etc. I have to visualize what being confident looks like, and fortunately, my wife is the perfect example. She can enter into a room and speak to everyone and anyone; she smiles and approaches people; I don't smile as broadly and often don't approach anyone.

Are you starting to see a pattern here?

Thus in all instances of goal setting, make sure you can visualize the actual item you wish to achieve; please do not say what you don't want, as you are merely recreating it, and as a result, will not change.

Always state what you want.

MY NOTES OR
THOUGHTS:

MY WISH LIST:

MY GOAL IS TO:

MY GOAL IS SMART:

SPECIFIC - MEASUREABLE - ATTAINABLE - REALISTIC - TANGIBLE

THE PLAN STEPS: DATES
NUMBER:

THE HURDLE/OBSTACLE IS?

POSSIBLE WAYS TO OVERCOME IT ARE?

THE HABITS I HAVE:

I WILL TRACK AS
FOLLOWS:

MY NOTES OR
THOUGHTS:

Acknowledgements

This book has been a challenge to myself, something I decided to test. I have kept it secret form the family, see above, but I have shared it with others who started a journey with me, and I would like to acknowledge these individuals, Roisin, Ilana, Neal, Pino, Doug - thank you.

To my family, while I did this in secret, I have to acknowledge you girls who brought me lunch when working even though I was not hungry, who shared experiences and smiled.

To my extended family, I hope the book sells enough for us to visit more often or I get invited to do some talks.

To every person I have worked with, the organisations I have worked in, the people on my linked-in profile, thank you.

To my clients, I have written this to learn but also show you, that anyone can achieve what they want, and I would like you to please go on and do this now.

About the Author

David will live to the age of 150 years and has some time remaining.

David is the founder and Managing Director of BeyondPossible, an organization aiming to take individuals and organizations beyond what they believe is possible.

He uses a blended approach that is customer-centric and is built around the materials of Leadership Management International, an organization that helps individuals reach their full potential. The products have been developed over 60 years and used in over 80 countries, translated into 23 plus languages, and have successfully impacted over two million individuals' development over this period. The Total Leadership Concept forms the foundation of the approach. It aims to ensure individuals can lead themselves in all areas of their lives, and manage their own time and priorities before leading and inspiring others.

You can read more about BeyondPossible and Leadership Management International using the below links.

The complementary approach is that of coaching, particularly business coaching, using the framework and methodology of South African Business Coaches, which has the goal to create more than 1000 Business Coaches who will help grow business for the benefit of all.

Coaching uses a non-directive approach, while Leadership Management materials provide a more directive approach to individual development; in combination, they have a synergistic effect.

As mentioned, David has climbed Kilimanjaro, ran a marathon, built a chuck box (If anyone wishes to enter into a partnership to build these commercially, please contact David).

David runs a successful business, lived, and worked in Nigeria, Saudi Arabia in multiple industries ranging from mining to oil and gas, consulting to retail. He holds numerous degrees, including an undergrad in Law and Philosophy, an

Honours Degree in Philosophy, and a Master of Business Administration. Countless short, courses sand certificates.

He is a member of various coaching bodies.

David and his family spend their time between South Africa and Croatia, as he is a dual national, and the plan is to coach in Croatia; you are helping achieve this.

His mission is to take a step every day towards a surreal life of joy, wealth, contribution, and adventure – and thanks to you for contributing to this, both in the writing of this book and for purchasing the book and also leaving a review.

What is next?

Another book is already in the making, the Camino in Europe and Japan, travel, coaching clients, and growing the world.

Sneaking this in - I will also be getting my Doctorate once I can convince my wife that I can study again – if I cannot convince her, guess I could do it in secret.

You can follow my progress and also visit his profiles using the below links:

www.beyondpossible.co.za

https://www.linkedin.com/in/david-davis-business-improvement-specialist-3a005a11/

https://www.sabusinesscoaches.co.za/david-davis/

---

[i] The first known use of SMART was in November 1981 in the Management Review, by George T Doran, according to Wikipedia.
[ii] How to Measure Anything: Finding the Value of Intangibles in Business – Douglas W. Hubbard.
[iii] Competence Refined: The 5 Components of Competence – Dr. Elana Siew.
[iv] The Obstacle if the Way – Ryan Holiday and Tim Ferris.

Made in the USA
Las Vegas, NV
14 February 2021